The Parish Special Constables Scheme

by
Peter Southgate
Tom Bucke
Carole Byron

A Research and Planning Unit Report

Home Office
Research and
Statistics
Department

London: Home Office

Home Office Research Studies

The Home Office Research Studies are reports on research undertaken by or on behalf of the Home Office. They cover the range of subjects for which the Home Secretary has responsibility. Titles in the series are listed at the back of this report (copies are available from the address on back cover). Other publications produced by the Research and Planning Unit include Research Findings (which are summaries of research projects), the Research Bulletin (published twice each year) and the annual Research Programme.

The Research and Statistics Department

The Department consists of the Research and Planning Unit, three Statistics Divisions, the Programme Development Unit and the Economics Unit.

The Research and Statistics Department is an integral part of the Home Office, serving the Ministers and the department itself, its services, Parliament and the public through research, development and statistics. Information and knowledge from these sources informs policy development and the management of programmes; their dissemination improves wider public understanding of matters of Home Office concern.

First published 1995

Application for reproduction should be made to the Information Section, Research and Planning Unit, Home Office, 50 Queen Anne's Gate, London SW1H 9AT.

Foreword

In 1993 the Home Secretary announced the widespread establishment of 'Parish Constable' schemes in rural areas. These schemes - now extended throughout the country and included as part of the 'Neighbourhood Constable' initiative - involve the allocation of trained Special Constables to specific local areas. Their main tasks are to provide a foot patrol presence and to address problems of nuisance and minor crime. The overall aims are to increase communication between the police and rural communities and to enhance community involvement in law and order issues.

The Home Office Research and Planning Unit undertook to study four schemes in detail during the first six months of their existence and to collect information from a dozen or more other schemes around the country. The focus of interest was the organisational strengths and weaknesses of the schemes and the factors which contributed to these. The researchers listened to the views and experiences of a wide range of people from the police and local communities and this report explores various aspects of the schemes. It concludes with a discussion of the progress made during 1994 and makes a number of recommendations on how schemes could be strengthened in the future.

ROGER TARLING

Head of Research and Planning Unit

Acknowledgements

We are most grateful to all those who helped us during the course of this study. A great many people were involved, both in the Derbyshire, Dorset, Kent and North Yorkshire schemes and in a number of others around the country. Although there are too many individ-uals to thank by name, particular thanks should go to those who were actually working as Parish Special Constables. The information, views and experiences which all these people passed on to us provided the substance of the account which follows.

We should also like to thank Tim Grosvenor and Malcolm Scott who conducted discussion groups with residents in the various scheme areas.

PETER SOUTHGATE
TOM BUCKE
CAROLE BYRON

Contents

Summary

Towards the end of 1993 the Home Secretary announced that he would like to see at least 20 'Parish Constable' schemes established, for a minimum of six months in the first instance. Such schemes would involve the allocation of trained Special Constables to specific local areas, where their main activities would be providing a foot patrol presence and addressing problems of nuisance and minor crime. Other tasks might include crime prevention advice, schools liaison, victim support and advice to watch schemes. The schemes were intended to encourage forces to communicate more with and be more responsive to the concerns of local communities, and to encourage communities to feel a sense of responsibility for and involvement with law and order and policing issues.

An alternative approach, encouraged as part of the same initiative, was to appoint 'Parish Wardens'. Wardens were to address similar problems on behalf of their communities but would not be members of the police service and would have no police powers of arrest. They would, in general, act as channels for information and advice between the police and the community.

Police forces and local authorities were invited to find suitable communities and individuals to fill Parish Constable and Parish Warden posts, and the Home Office Research and Planning Unit (RPU) was asked to study as many of the schemes as possible. It would then report on the experience of the first six months of the schemes, assessing the strengths and weaknesses of their organisation and identifying factors which contributed to these.

Initially, about half the police forces in England expressed interest in setting up a Parish Constable scheme. Twenty schemes were identified which were based upon the redeployment and/or recruitment of Special Constables into Parish Special Constable (PSC) work. One further scheme - organised by a local authority and using Parish Wardens - then joined the groups to be studied by RPU.

Of the 20 original schemes two dropped out at an early stage, and several others provided very little information about their progress. But across England and Wales as a whole the number of places known to have set up or shown interest in a PSC scheme has now grown to several hundred. During the course of 1994, the concept of the *Parish* Constable was subsumed into that of the *Neighbourhood* Constable. The intention is that the contribution of volunteer constables should be developed to cover a range of situations, of which the rural parish is but one.

The RPU study focused upon four schemes. These were in Ironville in Derbyshire, Pembury in Kent, Sleights in North Yorkshire and Yetminster in Dorset. This gave a range of small and large schemes, with a varied socio-economic profile and good geographical spread. In Dorset a Warden scheme set up at Stalbridge by the County Council was also monitored.

In each scheme information was gathered on: local policing demands and activities; how the scheme had been planned, established and run; and the views of local police officers, councillors and residents. This information came from: (i) documents from and interviews with the organisers of the schemes; (ii) interviews with people living or working in each locality (Regular police officers, PSCs, Parish Council members, other local figures); (iii) public attitude surveys organised locally; (iv) discussion groups conducted in each area by a research agency commissioned by RPU.

Although the hope was that the first group of PSC schemes would start by the beginning of 1994, many schemes only really became fully established later in the year, as considerable time was often needed to plan and set up a soundly-based scheme. Thus, some had not achieved full implementation by the end of 1994. Even for schemes which did start early, though, it is important not to make premature judgements about their success or failure: such initiatives take time to bear fruit; a view endorsed by all those involved in the schemes.

Of the four PSC schemes examined in detail during 1994, one has now closed down and three continue; and the one Parish Warden scheme failed to survive. The report describes each scheme and comments on why it survived or failed to do so. Drawing upon the information gathered from these and various other schemes it provides information and comments upon a range of issues. These include:

- The policing priorities of local communities

- The terms of employment of PSCs

- The objectives and features of PSC schemes

- The role of Parish Councils

- Recruitment and training

- The management and supervision of PSCs

- Links with the Regular force

- Patrol visibility and activity patterns

- Local reactions to PSC schemes

- PSCs and proactive policing tasks.

Most of the report concentrates upon Parish Special Constable schemes, but it also offers some observations about the one Parish Warden scheme which was examined. Other responses to law and order problems are also discussed including the 'Community Force' run by one local council, private security firms, and a 'streetwatch' scheme using neighbourhood 'Observers'.

In its concluding chapter, the report emphasises the importance of getting the right sort of people involved in the work; the difficulties which PSCs can face in defining a role for themselves within a community; the perceived policing needs of communities, and their reactions to the schemes; and the importance of proper integration between PSCs and the rest of their police force.

The report concludes with a series of recommendations, designed to strengthen existing schemes and guide the establishment of future schemes. These include:

- Parish Councils must be given adequate time to consult their communities before a scheme is established.

- The public must be given realistic information about how much time PSCs will be able to provide, what their legal powers will be and what they may or may not be able to achieve. People must know how to contact their PSC, and how the PSC can relay information to the Regular police force.

- PSCs cannot perform effectively if they are recruited directly into the work without adequate training and preparation. Normally, they will need to have spent some time in the Special Constabulary before they undertake PSC work.

- PSC work demands a lot of a volunteer, and great care must be taken to get the right sort of people into the job. Only those interested in and suited to the community side of policing rather than incident-response work should be considered as PSCs.

- Supervisors should try to maximise the time which PSCs spend on foot patrol and in direct contact with their community. More patrol during daylight hours would increase visibility, and this might, in turn, increase public reassurance.

- PSCs working alone in a village need particularly strong support and encouragement to avoid becoming isolated. Closer integration is needed between PSCs and the Regular force, particularly local beat officers.

- PSCs could also benefit from more contact with other Specials. It is important here to build upon existing Special Constabulary supervision and management structures, strengthening and developing these as necessary.

- In the longer term, the way to improve PSC patrol coverage and continuity of staffing, while reducing the demands on individual volunteers, could be to set up a small team of PSCs in a village. It might also be productive to rotate Specials between PSC and traditional section work, so as to strengthen links with the rest of the Regular force and the Special Constabulary.

- Before getting involved in crime prevention advice, Neighbourhood Watch or other proactive tasks, PSCs must be established in their patrol work and have received some specialist training. This will take time.

- PSCs must have adequate means of radio and telephone communication with the local control room.

- Where possible, PSCs should have a local base from which to work. The premises should be well maintained and clearly identified as a police office, so as to present a favourable public image.

- The longer term impact of PSC schemes upon crime, disorder and public perceptions of policing needs to be monitored.

1 Introduction

Background

In recent years law and order has become an increasing concern in rural areas. This has been for two main reasons. First, it was realised that crime was happening not only in deprived urban areas, but also in more rural parts of the country; communities traditionally seen as peaceful and law-abiding became aware that they too were suffering from both property crime and crimes of personal violence. Although figures released in April 1993 showed that the national rate of increase in recorded crime had actually slowed down in 1992, there were large variations between police force areas (Home Office, 1993), and some press reports chose to focus upon these, emphasising the above-average rates of increase to be found in a few mainly rural counties.

Second, people in rural areas also became aware that the police resources available to them were very limited. These concerns, coupled with the disposal of police premises in villages, and various reorganisations in police service delivery helped encourage the widespread anxiety that resources for rural policing were being progressively reduced. Opinions vary as to whether the supposed 'golden age' of policing, with a foot patrol officer on every city corner and every village street, ever actually existed. But, like most such 'myths' the idea is probably based partly upon fact and partly upon wishful thinking.

Even if greater resources could be allocated, it is not clear how far the problems would be resolved. Although it has sometimes been found to reduce fear of crime there is little evidence that increased police patrol will, certainly in urban situations, actually reduce crime (Reiner, 1992). Rural police patrols have to cover much larger areas and more widely dispersed populations, and the likelihood of a patrol being in the right place at the right time to deter or respond to a crime or incident is, therefore, probably even less in rural areas than in towns.

If both the costs of policing and public expectations of the police continue to rise, then the level of dissatisfaction with the police seems unlikely to fall. It may be that rural areas have only recently caught up with urban areas in experiencing a gap between what the police are able to deliver and what the population wishes they would deliver.

After the media debate in 1993 about the law and order needs of rural communities, the Home Secretary invited suggestions from individuals, police forces and local authorities for the introduction of volunteer 'Parish Constables'. The panel set up to consider the replies recommended that two models should be tested: the Parish Special Constable and the Parish Warden, with characteristics drawn from a number of entries.

The Home Secretary announced that he would like to see 20 schemes at least, established for a minimum of six months, and police forces and local authorities were invited to find suitable communities and individuals. The Home Office Research and Planning Unit agreed to study as many of the schemes as possible, to assess their strengths and weaknesses and identify factors which contributed to these.

Definitions

Parish Special Constable (PSC) schemes were intended by the Home Office to:

- encourage forces to communicate with and be responsive to the concerns of local communities

- encourage communities to feel a sense of responsibility for and involvement with law and order issues and their policing needs

- encourage communities to assist the police with their knowledge and expertise of the local area.

In working to achieve these goals, the schemes were to have the following elements:

- a trained Special Constable

- an agreement between the police and Parish Council about the level of service to be provided

- an increased visible foot patrol presence

- addressing problems of nuisance, minor crime and victim support

- giving crime prevention advice

- schools liaison

- advice to watch schemes.

Parish *Warden* schemes were to be broadly similar in their aims, but would have the following features and elements:

- no police powers of arrest

- the Warden would represent the parish

- victim support

- crime prevention advice

- perceived 'special relationship' with the police

- passing on to the parish accurate information on: rules and procedures for the conduct of investigations and prosecutions, the reliance of the police upon the public, recommended behaviour at crime scenes

- obtaining accurate information for the parish on: progress of local investigations and criminal activity in the area

- to report to the police on: minor offences (vandalism etc.) and concerns about local criminal activity.

Take-up

Interest was expressed initially by about half the police forces in England, and 20 schemes were identified which followed the PSC model. These were all based upon the redeployment and/or recruitment of Special Constables into Parish Special Constable work. One further scheme - organised by a local authority and using Parish Wardens - then joined the groups to be studied by RPU.

Since then, the number of schemes in England and Wales has grown to over 200. Of the 20 original schemes, two have effectively dropped out and, at the time of writing (January 1995), several others have yet to provide sufficient information to justify any clear conclusions about their progress, although it is known that they have established PSC schemes.

During the course of 1994, the whole concept of *Parish* Constable was subsumed into that of *Neighbourhood* Constable. As such, the intention is that the contribution of volunteer constables should be developed in a range of situations, of which the rural parish is but one. The Parish Special

Constable thereby becomes, as it were, a special case of the Neighbourhood Constable. For purposes of this report the term Parish Special Constable (PSC) will be used, because it was this particular role which was under examination. It is not yet known what the broad pattern of response will be to the proposed change in terminology, but some forces will continue to use the 'Parish' prefix for rural schemes.

In addition to PSC or Warden schemes, there have been other experiments with volunteers helping to 'police' their local areas. In Lincolnshire, members of the public help to man the front desks of some rural police stations, effectively converting them into information offices and keeping them from closure. In Glenfield, Leicestershire the 'Observers' operate a scheme that conforms closely to the 'Street Watch' strand of the 'Partners Against Crime' initiative launched in September 1994. This three-pronged initiative seeks to encourage more members of the public to join Neighbourhood Watch, to take similar principles of observation out into the streets as Street Watch, and to join the Special Constabulary as a local Neighbourhood Special Constable.

Another scheme which should be mentioned is the Community Force at Sedgefield, Co Durham, where the district council has employed its own private security patrol. A report on public reactions to the Sedgefield scheme has been prepared at Sheffield University and is available separately.

The RPU report

The RPU was asked to report on the establishment and operation of the schemes during the first six months of their existence, looking in more detail at a small number of these. The emphasis was to be upon organisational aspects of the schemes; it was recognised that it would be impossible and, indeed, unwise to seek to judge the effectiveness of the schemes in other respects after such a relatively short time.

In principle, the period to be covered ran from the start of January to the end of June 1994, but a number of schemes took much longer than was originally hoped to establish themselves. Thus, although 20 PSC schemes had 'started' in some sense by Christmas 1993, this did not mean that PSCs were actually on patrol by that date. Most started patrol work between January and March 1994; some not until April or May. Some, although having appointed officers by about April, did not have people fully trained at that time and were not planning to reach that stage until much later in 1994, or even into 1995.

Thus, the various schemes were at very different stages of development by the summer of 1994. One of the four schemes studied in detail ceased operation at that time, while another had only recently started. As far as possible, therefore, this report takes account of information available up to the end of 1994. Apart from those with schemes being studied closely, only two or three forces kept RPU fully advised of their progress as requested at the start of the year. Judgement must, therefore, be reserved on their experiences until they have more to report.

The six months time-frame is not seen as crucial. The main objective is to provide an indication of how different schemes developed during the early part of their existence and what their strengths and weaknesses were. For this to be done it was not essential that they should all be at exactly the same point in their development. Indeed, in some respects it is instructive to consider why they were not.

Given the fairly short life of the schemes so far, it is not possible to say very much about any lasting effects upon their communities. 'Before and after' crime and incident figures were available for comparable periods in some cases, but the numbers were so small that it was not possible to identify real changes, or to draw conclusions about the impact of the schemes upon crime levels. In one scheme, for example, a total of 26 offences of any sort were recorded in the parish during its six-month life.

RPU attention was concentrated upon schemes in four areas: Ironville in Derbyshire, Pembury in Kent, Sleights in North Yorkshire and Yetminster in Dorset. In Dorset a Warden scheme set up by the County Council was also monitored. The areas were selected so as to give a range of small and large schemes, with a varied socio-economic profile and a good geographical spread. Kent and Derbyshire were both counties which had experienced above average recorded crime increases in 1992; the increase in North Yorkshire was around the average and Dorset was below average.

A variety of information was sought from these schemes. This covered: (a) the inception, organisation and operation of each scheme; (b) crime and incident figures; (c) activity and workload data; (d) the views of local residents.

The information came from a variety of sources: (i) documents from and interviews with the organisers of the schemes; (ii) interviews with people living or working in each locality (Regular police officers, PSCs, Parish Council members, other local figures); (iii) public attitude surveys organised locally; (iv) discussion groups conducted in each area by a research agency commissioned by RPU.

As often happens, the amount and quality of information available varied from scheme to scheme. Ideally, sample surveys might have been used to assess the nature of public attitudes towards crime, policing and the PSC schemes. But this was not done, because the cost of commissioning adequate survey work in all the areas would have been prohibitive. Some general advice and a draft questionnaire were, in fact, offered to all the schemes, and a total of nine forces ran surveys of some kind during the period of the study. They, in turn, had insufficient resources for very thorough survey work with the result that, with one or two exceptions, the surveys conducted so far have been somewhat weak in their sampling procedures. Several have relied upon residents to return a self-completion questionnaire delivered to doors by PSCs or local council members. Some produced response rates as low as one in ten, while others reached more respectable levels of four or six out of ten. Particularly with lower rates of response, these surveys cannot be regarded as fully representative of local opinion. Those who returned questionnaires will, on the whole, have been people with a relatively high level of awareness of the schemes and/or support for them; those not aware of the PSC scheme are less likely to have bothered to respond. Also, the samples achieved may be biased in demographic terms. The best way to use the survey results available is to regard them as indicative of the views of some local residents, but not to draw firm conclusions about the balance of such views within the community.

Individual interviews were conducted by RPU staff, while professional discussion group leaders with experience of policing research were engaged to conduct discussion groups among local residents. The groups were comprised of: young people, parents of young children, middle-aged people with older or no children, and elderly people. Each group had eight to ten people, selected randomly by research agency field staff. In addition to the group leader, a member of the RPU research team was also present at one or more of the sessions in each area. The atmosphere in the groups was relaxed and people appeared to talk freely and openly. The group leaders worked through the following issues, though many other points were also raised along the way by participants: local crime and disorder problems; fear of crime; policing priorities; visibility of / satisfaction with police; knowledge and views of PSC / Warden scheme; expectations of and priorities for the PSC / Warden.

The aim of this report is to describe the issues and problems which have arisen so far in PSC schemes, with a view to seeing how they can best be dealt with in planning future schemes. A number of the comments and observations are critical, but it was probably inevitable that mistakes would be made in setting up a new initiative of this kind over such a relatively short period of time. The point of any criticism is to identify lessons about how to improve things in the future. In most cases these lessons are fairly clear from the experiences which have been described. A central feature of the schemes is the fact that they rely upon volunteer personnel. There will always be specific challenges in the recruitment, management, training, motivation and supervision of volunteers, and future developments need to be seen in this light.

2 Progress of the schemes

The four areas

Ironville

The village:

Ironville is a village of about 1,000 situated in eastern Derbyshire. The towns of Alfreton and Ripley are between two and three miles away, while the county border with Nottinghamshire skirts the eastern edge of the village. Although set in a semi-rural location, Ironville differs in physical, economic and social respects from the other three scheme areas studied.

In the centre of Ironville is an area of 1970s terraced council housing, and a shopping precinct. Around this is further council housing, including C19th terraces, semi-detached retirement bungalows and modern terraced houses. On a hill in the southern part of Ironville is Codnor Park, an inter-war estate of semi-detached houses surrounded by a small amount of C19th accommodation and an increasing number of modern residences, including small semi-detached starter homes and large detached houses. Unlike the rest of the village, there is little council housing here, with the majority being owner-occupied. Ironville also has a Anglican church, church hall, primary school, nursery, community centre, youth centre, doctor's surgery and two working men's clubs. Commercial facilities include a public house, sub-post office/village store, fish and chip shop, turf accountant, newsagent, greengrocer and hairdresser.

The economic focus of Ironville used to be the industrial enterprises which led to the village's creation and which provided employment for its residents. However, over the last 25 years, the coal mine, carriage works, pipe works and iron/steel foundry have all closed; the demolition of the associated buildings means that there is now little evidence of their existence. A significant proportion of the village's current social housing was originally built by these enterprises and only became council owned at the point of their closure. Long-term unemployment is now a problem in Ironville, especially among the younger residents. Only the shops and a haulage firm now offer employment in the village, while limited prospects are provided by industrial estates in the area. Some residents are employed in Nottingham and Derby, but need their own transport in order to travel there. Overall, Ironville has a run-down feel about it, reflected in empty shops, boarded up or derelict houses, graffiti and vandalism.

Existing policing provisions:

Ironville, along with nine other parishes, forms part of the Alfreton Section, the largest in the Amber Valley Division in size, population and police numbers. The Section is commanded by an Inspector, who manages 34 officers on a four shift basis with, on average, one Sergeant and eight Constables per shift. There are no area beat officers; instead patrols cover the main population areas and respond as needed elsewhere. Until the PSC scheme began, Ironville was receiving rather limited police attention. This was attributed by the local police partly to staffing problems and partly to the fact that the village lies on the margins of the area; beyond this lay the territory of the Nottinghamshire Constabulary.

Until the mid-1980s, Ironville had a resident officer who lived in Codnor Park and operated a small office next door. Like a Rural Beat Officer he was responsible for a large area as well as Ironville, and was sometimes called into Alfreton to deal with emergencies. While this post no longer exists and the police house has been sold, the police office is still used by visiting Regular officers and by the PSCs.

A police officer has normally attended Parish Council meetings, which typically raise complaints about the racing of cars and motorbikes in the village, the vandalising of vacant council houses and the misuse of air guns.

Pembury

The village:

Pembury in Kent is a very different sort of place from Ironville. It has a fairly large population for a village *circa* 6,000. It lies three miles to the east of Tunbridge Wells and is often described as somewhat of a dormitory area, with a suburban rather than rural feel to it. There is quite a wide range of housing in the village but, in general, it is a fairly middle-class, not obviously wealthy area. Many people commute to Tunbridge Wells, Paddock Wood or Tonbridge or, via these places, to London. The 1960s and 1970s saw considerable expansion, with new estates being built around the parish, but in the last ten years there has been less development.

Until six years ago the village had a serious problem with through traffic, but most of this is now carried on by-pass roads to the southwest and north of the village. The main street through the village is still busy at times, but not with the constant streams of heavy traffic of earlier years.

There are a number of shops in the village (several of which sell alcohol). Nearby is Tunbridge Wells which provides a wide range and quality of retail outlets and other services. In Pembury there are three pubs, four take-away food outlets, a garage, a bank, post office and various other retail and commercial premises. The village has an Anglican and a Free Church and a wide range of voluntary and social groups.

Existing policing provisions:

Pembury comes within the Tunbridge Wells police area, and day-to-day policing is the responsibility of the Duty Inspector. At the time the PSC scheme was established this officer was based some 12 miles away from Pembury, at Cranbrook police station, though this arrangement has been under review. The Area Response Team of nine Regular police constables, based in Paddock Wood, provides cover for an area including Pembury and four other villages: Paddock Wood, Five Oak Green, Matfield and Brenchley. One of these officers does, in fact, live at Pembury and was at one time the Resident Beat Officer (RBO) for the village.

Two ex-police houses with a small office attached remain in a street fairly central to the village. Although any Police signs are removed the office is now, in fact, used by the PSCs. But it is the past rather than the present use of the buildings which residents seemed to be aware of, and their somewhat shabby state did not present the most favourable image of policing provision for the village to them.

In earlier days the RBO did live in one of these houses, though he has since moved elsewhere in the village. He was actually responsible for policing in Pembury for only 18 months, and for nearby Five Oak Green for another 18 months prior to that, but his was the name on the lips of most of those interviewed as the officer who personified the 'lost ideal' of village policing in Pembury. Although still a member of the area team, he now finds little if any time available to devote specifically to the needs of Pembury. He no longer contributes a column to the Parish Council magazine or keeps a file of information about incidents in the parish. Any contacts he has with Special Constables tends to take place in Paddock Wood rather than Pembury. There is, thus, no link between the PSCs and the regular police in Pembury through this particular channel.

As in other parts of the country, some people were unclear as to where their police service was based. Most looked to Tunbridge Wells, where the nearest police station is sited as well as being the area HQ.

Sleights

The village:

Sleights is four miles inland from Whitby on the North Yorkshire coast on the A169 Whitby to Pickering road. The village population is 2,382 while the parish which contains it - Eskdaleside-cum-Ugglebarnby - has a population of 2,872 (1991 census). It is on the edge of the North York Moors National Park, five miles from the village of Goatland, which features in the television series 'Heartbeat'. The image of rural policing presented in this series is very much to the fore in local thinking about policing.

Sleights is a combination of dormitory town, retirement village and holiday village. The housing reflects the social mix with an area: large houses in spacious grounds, holiday cottages, old housing, new private housing estates including bungalows, and a council estate which includes sheltered housing for old people. Sleights has a relatively high proportion of detached houses. The population comprises older retired people, families whose working members commute - to Whitby, Scarborough, York and Teeside, people whose families, often from farming backgrounds, have lived there over several generations, plus newcomers who have been housed on the council estate by Scarborough Borough Council.

Public transport is poor, but car ownership is high: only one in five households in Sleights is without a car and three out of ten households have two or more cars. The village has a post office, general store and newsagent, a butcher, two public houses, a fish and chip cafe, nursing homes, a modern doctors' surgery and a village hall.

The population is slightly older than that of Whitby and North Yorkshire: over one in four of the population are of pensionable age, and 44 per cent of households contain pensioners.

Existing policing provisions:

Regular policing cover in Sleights is provided by the Whitby Rural Area Team, one of five rural team areas within the Malton Division of North Yorkshire Police. Excluding Whitby town itself, the team area covers 250 square miles, ranging from Staithes in the North to Robin Hood's Bay in the South and Castleton in the West. The rural team works from Whitby Police Station and has an establishment of eight officers. During the period studied, however, there were, effectively, only five officers available to share the 24-hour rota.

Some former village police officers have bought what were the village police houses. This gives residents the impression that they have retained their own police officer. But Sleights felt it had lost its police officer as he had moved out of the police house. He is still a member of the rural team and continues to patrol as before, although he no longer attends school functions.

Each member of the team has responsibility for the whole area when on duty but has special responsibility for schools and pubs in a particular area. The mileage covered by rural team officers has increased (doubled, according to one officer) since the days of village police officers, but 24-hour cover is now available, manpower permitting. In addition, there is a traffic car on duty in the rural area, and Whitby Town Police also respond to emergencies. Thus, for the first six months of 1994, 58 per cent of incidents in Sleights were dealt with by police officers other than the rural team, 40 per cent by the rural team and two per cent by the PSC. This contrasts with the same period for 1993, when 63 per cent of incidents were dealt with by the rural team, possibly due to the temporary understaffing.

Previous cover by Specials:

In previous times, when Regular officers had their own village beats, Specials living near to them often went on duty with them on Friday or Saturday nights. When rural team policing was introduced in 1992 some Specials continued to do this. But, as rural team officers, the Regulars now had a beat which took them - and, thus, also the Specials - mostly outside the village. Residents then felt that they had lost not only their village police officer but also one or two Special Constables. The PSC at Sleights has been a Special for six years, working mainly in Whitby, before the PSC scheme. He had done occasional patrols in the village, so was not totally unfamiliar with his new assignment.

Yetminster

The village:

Yetminster is a small village located in a rural area of north-west Dorset with a population of just over 1,000. The parish includes Yetminster and the nearby hamlet of Rhyme Intrinseca which has 200 inhabitants. The nearest town in Dorset is Sherborne where the local police are based. A similar distance over the Somerset county boundary is the larger town of Yeovil. Yetminster is mentioned in the Doomsday Book and once was a rural farming community. The centre today is made up of residential stone houses, some with thatched roofs and many dating back to the early C18th. On the periphery of this is a patchwork of residential housing from different periods, including a few Victorian dwellings, some social housing built during the middle of this century and a large amount of recent development. The latter has affected both the demography and the visual character of Yetminster. It includes private housing, ranging from semi-detached starter homes, to large executive houses and bungalows inhabited by the retired. The building of further housing has increasingly become an issue with residents and the Parish Council: many feel that there has been too much building already and that the village is in danger of being spoilt. However, efforts have been made to preserve its character, with a number of new houses built in stone and the Council deciding not to introduce street lighting to the village centre.

Yetminster has a wide range of commercial outlets and public services. There is a village store with an off-licence, a greengrocer, a butcher, a hairdresser, two pubs, a guest house and a garage providing motor repairs and petrol. Other public facilities include a primary school, a doctor's surgery with three general practitioners, a veterinary surgeon and a post office. The village contains a Methodist and a very old Anglican church, there is also a bus service and a railway station with trains to Yeovil and Weymouth. Finally, a group of workshops are situated by the railway station containing businesses such as builders, engineers, printers, joiners and carpenters. Yetminster has a mixed population including a large number of retired people. There are some manual workers and a number of people who commute to London, while others travel to Yeovil, Sherborne or other nearby towns in Dorset or Somerset.

Existing policing provisions:

The western division of Dorset Police covers 600 square miles or two-thirds of Dorset. Each of its eight sections has between 12 and 15 officers and, usually, three police stations. Yetminster is in the Sherborne section, which is commanded by an Inspector based at the police station in Sherborne town.

Yetminster is served by a Rural Beat Officer (RBO), based at Sherborne and responsible for 15 villages and hamlets. He is an experienced officer with a good level of local contact. He and two other RBOs based at Sherborne form the Rural Police Team, rotating their duties between shifts and covering each others' areas as well as their own. This system allows them to share one police car.

The RBO for Yetminster, therefore, has to spend a great deal of his time outside the area. He tries to do foot patrol there as often as possible, since this led to better relations with residents and to useful information being received. He tries to attend all the Parish Council meetings in his area, amounting to five or six each month, often attended when off duty. Compared to other parts of the Sherborne section, Yetminster is considered by local officers to be well policed.

Before 1971 Yetminster was policed by an officer who lived in the village, though was also responsible for a number of other parishes. He had the freedom to adjust his hours of work but was, in effect, on call 24 hours a day while in his house. This meant he worked about 25 per cent more time than officially required. He patrolled by motorcycle and had little contact with the police station at Sherborne, except when called in to help police large public events or cover for other officers. After 1971 he was moved into Sherborne and the police house became a private residence.

In the recent past Yetminster had a very similar scheme to the PSC one: under 'Adopt-a-Village' two Special Constables from Sherborne were allocated to patrol the village on a regular basis. The scheme did not last long; there were problems over travelling expenses and the Specials involved found patrolling only in the village rather limiting.

Some Yetminster residents were unsure where their nearest police station was or where they were policed from. This may be partly due to the proximity of the Somerset county boundary and the fact that emergency calls are routed to Yeovil. A number of residents perceived the police to be remote from Yetminster, with the closing at night of the station in Sherborne cited as an example of the lack of policing in the area.

Yetminster's RBO or 'local community policeman' was well-known by residents and seen as quite active in the village. He seemed best known by middle-aged residents: some older people expressed a feeling of isolation from the police in general and wanted a more direct local service from them. But those with recent experience described the police as reasonably helpful and were general satisfied with their performance.

Local policing priorities

Residents in all the areas complained about varying degrees of incivility and disorder from teenagers in their village. Although the problems seemed to come and go over time the manifestations were much the same: disorderly gatherings; vandalism, both minor and major; and insulting behaviour towards any adults who tried to reprimand them. The offenders were normally described as ranging widely in age: anywhere between 8- and 17-years old. Street furniture of various kinds seemed to be a popular focus of attention: telephone boxes, post boxes, gates and fences, roadside mirrors, bus shelters etc. A bus shelter in Pembury, for example, was said to be used as a football goal, a canvas for graffiti, for setting fire to, for taking away as firewood and as a general gathering point. In Ironville, too, there was considerable vandalism to shops and houses, and some people claimed that gangs roamed the streets and waste grounds at night, lighting bonfires.

Some people saw these gangs as responsible for more serious crimes such as burglary, but others said this was perpetrated by more hardened criminals. Crimes such as burglary and car theft were often attributed to 'outsiders', usually from the nearest town of any size, sometimes in the next county. Thus, in Sleights, offenders were said to come from Teesside; in Yetminster from Yeovil or Bristol; in Pembury from towns in Kent or from London. Each village had one or more 'problem' families whose supposed misdemeanours ranged from providing the ringleaders for the teenage gangs, through committing the burglaries and car thefts, into drug and firearms dealing and use.

Where levels of local villainy were known to be of the latter order, neither police nor public felt it appropriate for the PSC to be involved: this became a job for the Regulars, probably the CID. This illustrates a dilemma as to how far involved in local crime problems the PSC can and should be. A sound knowledge of the local community is one thing, but involvement with armed criminals is another.

One or two villages were very conscious of some particular serious crime which had taken place there, and which tended to colour local views on crime and policing issues. Sleights had recently seen a murder take place during the course of a burglary. The offender had been convicted and imprisoned, and other local criminals had also been imprisoned for burglary offences. For the present, order had returned, but some residents were very concerned about what might happen when the offenders were released again into their midst. (Some of the offenders have now been released, but no further troubles have so far been recorded.)

Of the sites examined in detail, Ironville seemed to have some of the worst problems. It was physically and socially very different from the more 'typical' rural areas examined elsewhere, and its problems - of industrial decline, dereliction, unemployment and crime - were, in many ways, much closer to those of the inner city than of the country. The residents felt that the police were not doing enough to respond to their problems; some were sceptical that the local police could do very much to improve the crime situation in the area.

Terms of employment of PSCs

PSCs were normally employed on similar terms and conditions to other Special Constables who worked in the traditional way on sections. A few forces made an explicit distinction between the two roles, saying that individuals could not expect to change between the two. The most important distinction is that PSCs are supposed to spend all their time on duty working in a specific local area, whereas section Specials may be sent to various places as the need arises. In some schemes one person was appointed as PSC, while in others there may be several PSCs, possibly working in an informal rota. Like other Specials, PSCs have normal police powers of arrest, though they are not expected to respond to serious crimes but to concentrate upon community liaison and crime prevention work. Their main tasks are to provide a visible police presence and act as a channel of communication between the regular police and the community.

In some places the idea of Specials focusing their efforts on a particular local area was not seen as novel, having been tried before under another name. One scheme had, in fact, had a previous incarnation under a different title, but had been closed down, apparently because the Specials found it lacking in interest. In another area, an account was given of a Special who had been acting as the de facto PSC of a particular village for years, though not under that name.

Objectives and features of the schemes

The three broad objectives set for PSC schemes were: (a) the improvement of communication with local communities and response to their concerns; (b) the encouragement of feelings of community responsibility for and involvement with law and order issues and policing needs; and (c) encouraging communities to assist the police with their local knowledge. These can be summarised as the development of a 'partnership' approach between the police and local communities.

After only 6 to 12 months it would have been unrealistic to look for conclusive evidence of success or failure in achieving these objectives. What could usefully be examined, though, is what had been done organisationally to work towards them. This examination provides a range of organisational lessons for the future of existing schemes and for the establishment of new ones.

The role of Parish Councils

The original intention was that Parish Councils should play a key role in the development of PSC schemes. They were regarded as the formal channels for the needs and views of local residents, and one way in which the Home Office tried to emphasise the importance of police - community partnership was to suggest the drawing up between police forces and Parish Councils of written documents called 'Service Level Agreements'. These would set out the main features of a PSC scheme, provide realistic expectations of what the scheme might deliver, and make some visible commitment on both sides. Both parties would sign them.

Such agreements do not, so far, appear to have been particularly popular: none of the four forces studied used them in the form envisaged. Some forces made it a deliberate policy to delay having them until they had built up more experience of what the scheme could promise. Others drew them up immediately, though with modest aims which did not make too ambitious a commitment on their behalf. In one area there was such haste to set up an agreement (to meet what was, mistakenly, believed to be a Home Office deadline) that it was only realised later that the PSC himself had not been invited to sign it. Concern was also expressed from those involved in this scheme that not enough time had been allowed for the Parish Council to consult local residents before signing such an agreement.

In all schemes, though, even where there was no formal service agreement, there was some public statement of what the purpose of the scheme was, how it would operate and what it would hope to achieve. The police normally drew up a statement of what they hoped the PSC would do and how the scheme would be organised, and then presented this for discussion and agreement to the council or to key members of it. In Sleights, for example, the role of the PSC was described as primarily to provide a foot patrol and obvious presence in the village, dealing with instances of nuisance, minor crime and victim support. In response to misleading information in the media it was emphasised that there would be no withdrawal of other police cover, and that the PSC's work was complementary to that the Rural Team.

The Sleights Parish Council was told that "the sole controlling agency for the PSC will be the North Yorkshire Police, from whom he will receive his operating instructions". The Chair and Parish Council members confirmed that they did not think it was appropriate for them to set priorities for the PSC. They saw the role as being part of the police service which was quite separate from the role of the Parish Council.

Parish Council meetings were attended by PSCs in all schemes, though not on every occasion. In one case, there was some lack of clarity as to how often PSC attendance was expected: at one point each side seemed to be waiting for the other to suggest it. All councils expressed their support, though few went so far as to provide any financial backing. Even where councils were most supportive, their financial commitment was limited, amounting, perhaps, to no more than the purchase of a torch on behalf of the PSC. But other assistance given included the provision of the village hall for a meeting, and providing and distributing posters and leaflets.

In their meetings and in discussions with RPU, Parish Council members generally raised the same sorts of questions about PSC schemes as did other local residents: what training PSCs would have; what hours they would work; how they could be contacted; and what they would do about local crime and disorder.

Recruitment and training

Recruitment

The training and experience of the PSCs encountered in this study varied considerably. Some forces made it clear that they saw PSCs as separate from mainstream Specials, and were explicit that their jobs were not interchangeable. Mostly, though, the first thing which had been done in setting up PSC schemes was to trawl the experienced Specials to see which of them was (a) living in a suitable rural community and/or (b) willing to take on a PSC job. A degree of gentle 'persuasion' was used in some instances, though in others a suitable willing volunteer was more easily located. 'Suitable' meant, in this instance, a person of more mature years - and, more importantly, of mature outlook - not longing to become a regular officer and not concerned about the more 'exciting' aspects of Specials work, such as patrolling urban streets on weekend evenings.

Having exhausted this avenue, forces then set about actively recruiting new people into the Specials, with the specific purpose of staffing PSC schemes. Kent, for example, by the end of its initial campaign, had recruited and allocated 20 PSCs, these being a mixture of serving and newly-recruited Specials, mostly the latter.

Training methods

The training of any Special Constables normally takes place in two main ways: through regular classroom training sessions, typically of two hours once every two weeks; and through supervised patrol in the company of either experienced Regulars or Specials.

The challenge for many new recruits has been that, not only are they new to the work of policing, but that the role of PSC is itself an innovation. They have had to learn to be Specials and, at the same time, to develop into the newly defined role of PSC. This has not been easy, and for this reason it was not possible for some schemes to go fully 'live' as soon as they might have wished. Schemes have, therefore, come on stream at different times during the year, or they have used both experienced Specials and new recruits to work in one village.

Gaining experience

It was generally seen as important that a commitment be made to keep PSCs in their home village, and not take them away to make up the numbers for large public events and the like. But, in practice, some forces have had to violate this principle. This is because, in order to become fully qualified Specials, PSCs need to gain a wider range of experience than can be achieved simply by working in their own village: if they remain there it may well be a long time before they become competent to handle a wide range of situations. The danger is then that, if they are seen by local people to be inexperienced, this will confirm the suspicion - which came out strongly in some discussion groups - that PSCs are not 'real' Specials, let alone 'real' police officers.

Some PSCs have, thus, found themselves drafted into nearby towns on Friday and Saturday evenings in addition to patrolling their own village. Not only does this help them broaden their experience base, and achieve 'fully trained' status more quickly, but it provides a little more variety than foot patrol in the village.

The only obvious way round this problem seems to be to ensure that only experienced and qualified Special constables are appointed as PSCs. Failing this, every scheme needs at least one such person as part of its team, while newer recruits gain some of their experience elsewhere. If this cannot be achieved, then it seems advisable either to delay the official start of the scheme until the newly recruited PSC is adequately trained and experienced, or to phase in his/her exposure to the community very carefully. However, in forces which wish to keep their PSCs completely separate from other Specials, some form of purpose built PSC training programmes may need to be considered.

Place of PSCs' residence

The PSCs in Sleights and most of those in Pembury lived in the village, while those in Ironville and Yetminster did not. The question of how easy it should be for local residents to gain access to PSCs at times when they are not actually on duty is a difficult one. There are arguments on either side here, and these are considered a little later. A further aspect to this question was raised in Ironville. Here, although residents subscribed to the notion of a locally resident PSC, both the police and the Parish Council felt that it was acceptable for PSCs to live elsewhere, so that they did not get personally embroiled in any of the more hostile conflicts which might arise between residents over law and order issues.

Management and supervision

There was some variation between schemes in the extent to which they involved the existing Special Constabulary hierarchy of management and supervision. In all cases the Regular force was active in planning and setting up the schemes, and in monitoring them in the longer term. In some schemes, though, including Sleights and Yetminster, day-to-day supervision was then also carried out by Regular supervisors. The Sleights PSC reported directly to the Regular police and did not operate within the Specials' structure, although continuing to attend Specials' training sessions. In Pembury, there was fairly close involvement of both Regular and Special supervisors.

Initial responsibility for setting up the Ironville scheme appears to have fallen to the Divisional Commander and his Specials Liaison Officer and to the Divisional Commandant of the Special Constabulary. Job and skill profiles were written for all Parish Constable positions and a Parish Constable Liaison Officer appointed, with the SC rank of Section Officer, to coordinate all three schemes in Amber Valley. After this, though, the scheme was largely run by senior Specials. No formal link between Regular officers and Parish Constables was created. The PSCs reported to the Section Officer who, in turn, reported to the SC Assistant Divisional Commandant.

Links with the Regular force

Good communication between PSCs and Regulars is an issue, in its various aspects, which is central to the effective operation of PSC schemes if they are to play a meaningful part in the overall work of the police. There are interpersonal, organisational and technical aspects of communication which need to be considered.

Where the Special Constabulary has only limited involvement in running a scheme, there seems to be a danger of other Specials feeling they are being excluded from the initiative. In Sleights, some people in the Specials were under the impression that the PSC was being kept apart from them as the result of some Home Office policy. They felt they knew little about the scheme because it was operated separately through the Regular force. It was suggested that perhaps senior Specials should be involved by going on patrol with the PSC occasionally. While it may be necessary for the Regular force to take the first steps in planning and setting up PSC schemes, the support and involvement of the Special Constabulary is clearly vital if they are to be sustained over the longer term. Good working liaison between Regulars and PSCs at all rank levels is vital to the morale and effectiveness of PSCs.

One of the key roles envisaged for PSCs was to act as a link between their parish and the Regular police. A flow of information in both directions was intended to develop, to the benefit of all parties. For this to happen there must be effective working links between PSCs and the rest of the organisation, and PSC work must mesh in with that of full-time police officers. But these working links do not necessarily establish themselves automatically, and specific steps may have to be taken to ensure that PSCs are properly integrated into the work of the rest of the force. A variety of questions arise here. How are PSCs to be provided with up-to-date information about crime and other matters within their parish? How do they convey information from the public back to their force? How is the work of PSCs and Regular officers to be integrated into coherent policing strategies, and how are tasks shared between them within the parish?

Various practical means are used to exchange information between the Regular force and PSCs. Information exchange is tied in with arrangements for supervision, and there may be a mixture of links involved. In Pembury, for example, the PSCs have various lines of communication and supervision. The policing of the village is the responsibility of a Rural Area Inspector, based at a police station some twelve miles away (though this arrangement was under review at the time of writing), assisted by Regular Constables who patrol the area from various other bases. The PSCs' immediate supervisor is the Specials Section Officer and, above him, the Area Officer. These officers keep a record of the hours the PSCs work and help with their training needs. Overall responsibility for the work of PSCs in the area lies with an Inspector located at the area HQ.

When the PSCs book on for duty they ring the area control room. Information is fed to them via their office in the village by the Inspector at area HQ. This officer sends information to the PSCs every day or two via a civilian driver who updates a special loose leaf folder with any relevant new information for the PSCs to refer to. They also receive information on new crimes and incidents in the area via a fax located in the office. The PSCs in turn leave a note in the folder of any activity or incident which may be of interest, either to their colleagues in the village or to the Regular police. They return by post to the area HQ any paperwork they raise. There is also a 'Voicebank' of recorded messages which the PSCs are expected to call when they go on duty.

In Sleights, the PSC phones in to Whitby Police Station when he goes on duty and is given messages left for him by the public via the Police Station. The Duty Officer will also inform the PSC of any incidents which may need follow up, such as victim support work. As such messages and information are received they are placed in a special in-tray so that all information for the PSC is available in one place. No one individual appears to have specific responsibility for liaison with him, although the Specials Liaison Officer has contacted him occasionally. When he is on duty, he calls in to Whitby Police Station on the radio hourly so that they know where he is working.

An earlier study of Special Constables found a problem of trust and communication between Regular and Special officers (Mirrlees-Black and Byron, 1994). While some Regulars say they could not manage without their colleagues in the Specials, there were still Special Constables whom the authors talked to or were told about who had apparently suffered some overt resentment from Regulars. The term "hobby bobby" still appears to be in use and, even if used in jest by Regulars, it illustrates a basic scepticism about the abilities, commitment and general credibility of the Special Constable. There were PSCs who were reluctant to go for training with certain Regulars because they knew they were regarded with this scepticism.

In one of the scheme areas there was ill feeling about PSCs amongst some Regular officers, who felt that the scheme had been planned elsewhere and then presented to them as a 'fait accompli'. This feeling probably reflects the fact that the choice of location had been strongly influenced by the views of the county Association of Parish and Town Councils. Also, the responsibility for planning it was initially given to an Inspector from outside the division, and some time elapsed before most local officers were informed about the plans. Some of them felt that there were other places in the section which needed a PSC more.

In another area too there was some initial ill feeling from Regulars when the PSC scheme was first announced. This was related to the way they saw their own involvement. An idea originally proposed was that PSCs would form a team which would work with and support one or more Resident Beat Officers (RBOs). If manpower had allowed, the ideal might have been to have one RBO responsible for the village (or a small number of villages) who relied upon locally-based PSCs to do much of the work there. But things did not, in fact, happen in this way. In a rather unfortunate piece of timing, the RBO system was withdrawn. For some time demands on the RBOs had been such that their traditional 'village bobby' role had been difficult to fulfil, and they could no longer provide adequate foot patrol cover because there were so many abstractions and calls for assistance outside the villages where they lived. It was decided to recognise this fact by reorganising them into Area Response Teams. These teams still provide cover for all villages, but on a mobile, response basis.

Around the same time that these changes were being instituted the PSC schemes were set up. Not surprisingly, some of the ex-RBOs saw the two changes as directly linked and felt that they had been displaced by the PSCs. Thus, instead of supporting and collaborating with the PSCs, some of the area officers tended to withdraw even further from involvement with village policing than they had already been forced to do by the pressure of work elsewhere. This reduced their willingness to train the PSCs in the villages. Also, if they do take out inexperienced PSCs this may mean going out in cars, and away from the village as they respond to calls over the wider area they now police.

It should be accepted that some resistance to PSC schemes may be encountered from Regular officers, and may be provoked for a variety of reasons. Care is needed to anticipate these sensitivities and avoid introducing schemes in ways which seem to ignore the concerns or experience of Regular officers. They need to be involved in the development of such new initiatives, and they need to work closely with the PSCs if an atmosphere of trust and cooperation is to develop. In the first instance, the training aspect of such relationships will need to be emphasised. Then, later on, PSCs will need to have good working contact with Regular force members if they are to fulfil their role as a link between the police force and the community.

The situation of the *Parish* Special Constable creates a particular problem here. Section Specials traditionally gain a lot of their experience by working alongside the Regulars. But the PSC role is much more isolating: in demanding that the PSCs should work all - or almost all - of their time in their designated village, it virtually ensures that they will gain only a narrow range of experience and have limited contacts with the Regular force.

There were examples of PSCs who were working in relative isolation from the rest of their force but were fairly happy with this state of affairs: they knew their village well and were developing their own style of 'policing' it. In some ways this may work quite effectively: the PSCs gain experience relevant to the work they need to do for most of their time, and develop an approach very close to what was envisaged for them. Without a broader range of policing experience and fuller exposure to the Regular force, though, they will not easily be absorbed into the organisational culture and working practices of that wider organisation. They may then have a difficult task in convincing the more hardened Regulars that they should be regarded as 'real' police officers to be consulted about and involved in local policing issues.

PSCs are not, of course, expected to be involved in serious crimes; and emergencies tend, in any case, to be reported direct to the police HQ via a 999 call. It is not uncommon for response vehicles or specialist squads to be deployed without local beat officers - including PSCs - being involved at all. However, if PSCs are not seen by their community to be adequately informed about local law and order issues, then their credibility with the community may suffer. Cases were mentioned where PSCs had only received information about a local crime or incident several days after it occurred. It had caused some embarrassment when a query from the public was the first they knew of the incident. When one Parish Council wrote to the police pointing out the importance of their keeping the PSC informed of incidents which might require his follow-up they were told that the PSC controls his own duty time and the police did not wish to impose upon his personal time. Nevertheless, this particular PSC felt that the flow of information to him had improved as time went on.

If local people find that their PSC is poorly informed about local incidents the suspicion may be confirmed in their mind that these officers are, indeed, not 'real' police officers.

Unfortunately, a person who is working only, say, four hours a week as a police officer may well have difficulty in keeping fully in touch with all relevant policing issues and practices.

There were some PSCs who were distinctly uneasy about the isolated situation in which they found themselves. There is, perhaps, an important difference here between those who work as one of a small group of PSCs working in one parish, as in Pembury, and those who work alone, as in Sleights. Even though some Section Specials complain about isolation from Regulars, they do normally have the companionship of other Specials. Much of the satisfaction of voluntary work does, after all, come from such companionship. But many PSCs are doubly isolated: first, they are removed from other Specials, and then put into a new job in which they may suffer indifference, lack of contact and consultation, or even hostility from the Regulars upon whom they depend for their professional back-up. Fortunately, most Specials are fairly resilient and cheerful people who can cope with this, and not all want to be part of a team in any case.

There is a balance to be drawn here between the provision of a locally-based service, focused upon local needs and concerns, and the provision of a standard and style of policing which is consistent throughout the whole of a police force area. No great problems seem to have been encountered so far, but this is an issue which forces with PSCs working over extended periods in relative isolation will want to keep a close watch on.

Current organisational structures are such that either one or a team of Regular constables is responsible for routine police cover in any given place. One might, then, expect that this officer should work closely with the PSCs within his area, exchanging information with them on a day-to-day basis. One approach could be for the PSCs to be allocated to the Regular PC, so that he would use them as a resource, agreeing work times, patrol routes and priorities with them. He would be informed of - and, possibly, involved in -

the force response to any serious crimes in the local area, and he would, in turn, keep the PSCs up to date about these matters. This is an ideal model which seemed to be rare, though not unknown, in practice. The idea of having a team of PSCs as support for a local Regular beat officer had certainly been explored in one force but was, in the event, not taken up, somewhat to the dissatisfaction of the Regular officers concerned.

Technical issues:

A number of forces complained of technical problems in developing their PSC schemes, relating to poor radio reception in certain isolated areas. Police personal radios can sometimes only operate within close range of a patrol car radio acting as a repeater station, but few PSCs have such access. This means that they are not necessarily in direct radio contact with police control rooms. In some cases PSCs have been issued with mobile telephones instead of or, sometimes, as well as a radio, though this is not always seen as adequate.

Patrol visibility

Varying numbers of hours of PSC time were recorded in the different schemes. The average total numbers of officer hours worked per month in the various schemes were as follows:

Pembury	62	(5 PSCs)
Yetminster	20	(1-2 PSCs)
Sleights	30	(1 PSC)
Ironville	40	(1-2 PSCs)

Within individual schemes, there was considerable variation in the amount of time being put in. In some, one individual might put in as much as 35 hours in some months, while another did nothing. It seems likely that this will always be a problem with voluntary schemes; individual availability and commitment will vary from one person to another, so that exact working schedules may be difficult to plan in advance.

One test of what these hours achieve in terms of visible patrol is to conduct systematic surveys of local residents. North Yorkshire Police ran their own survey in Sleights which indicated that about two-thirds of those who responded - the response rate was just over half the target sample - said they had seen their PSC in the village. Even if the non-responders were all people who had *not* seen the PSC and people only responded to the survey if they *had,* then one can conclude that *at least* one in three residents had actually seen the PSC.

Further survey evidence on this point may yet become available, but these results seem encouraging. As the PSC himself pointed out, much of his patrol work - in the winter at least - was done in the dark when there were few people about to see him. The proportion who say they have seen him is probably, thus, an underestimate of his level of activity.

The question of when PSCs should patrol was raised in the discussion groups, and it was agreed that this was not straightforward. The evenings, especially Friday and Saturday around pub closing times, were seen by some people as the most important times for the PSC to be about, while others felt that many burglaries happened during the day and that this is when the PSC should patrol. There would, of course, be greater visibility - and thus, probably, increased public reassurance and satisfaction - if more time could be spent on daytime patrol. But this comes up against the problem of the availability of volunteers, many of whom have other job commitments during the day. Where possible, the solution to this might be to try to recruit PSCs with flexible schedules in their regular jobs.

Activity patterns

None of the four schemes studied were able to provide precise information on the use of time by their PSC, but the following list of activities from one of the schemes illustrates the range of PSC involvement.

The PSC concerned worked mostly on Tuesday, Friday or Saturday evenings. The bulk of his time was taken up with patrolling the village, when he would check the security of buildings and vehicles. Some further work stemmed from his patrol duties, either through observation or residents approaching him while on patrol. For example:

- Suspected burglary

- Lost property

- Lost dog

- Snow blocking main road through village

- Criminal damage to hedges, fence and garage wall

- Alarm operating in private house

- Van door found unlocked.

Other examples of work which stemmed from information given to him by the police station were:

- A resident concerned about knocking on her door in the early hours.

- Following observations on local coal yard where theft had taken place, a man was chased along the riverbank.

- Checks concerning car damage and children on bicycles with no lights.

- Right-of-way dispute.

- Bullying, youths setting dogs on cats and problems with children verbally abusing an adult.

Some work developed through information from the Parish Council such as:

- Visits to elderly people about various concerns e.g. gas meter found in garden.

- Parking on double yellow lines outside shop.

Other activities undertaken:

- Coding mountain bikes.

- Attending meetings of Parish Council, organising public meeting on crime prevention.

- Prize and badge-giving at local schools and Brownies.

- Press, television and radio interviews about the scheme.

In another scheme the original PSCs concentrated upon relaunching the Neighbourhood Watch scheme, spending a lot of their time leafleting the village and organising meetings. A later recruit to the scheme, however, focused far more upon patrolling the village and providing a visible police presence. In the Summer months special attention was said to have been given to:

- young motorcyclists who rode around the village and annoyed other residents;

- users of air guns who upset residents by carrying them openly in the village;

- 'strange' cars in the area or ones with no road tax;

- and the reservoir, just outside the village, where drug dealing was suspected.

A great deal of time was spent chatting to residents in the streets and the youths congregating around the shopping precinct.

One or two other forces provided fairly detailed records of how their PSCs' time was spent while on duty, and it is useful to consider these also as illustrative of PSC work patterns. The categories used vary somewhat, but the one-third of these schemes used a form of the Home Office RPU activity sampling method *(Home Office, 1992)*

Scheme 1	all time %	time in parish only %
Solo foot patrol	14	26
Accompanied foot patrol	5	9
Mobile patrol	20	37
Hunting events	14	25
Parish Council meetings	2	3
Work outside parish	46	-
	(164 hours)	(89 hours)

Based on: 164 hours duty over 26 weeks
(= 6.3 hours per week on average)

The PSC in this scheme was clearly not spending all his time on work within the parish. Nor, indeed, did some others. In one it was common for the PSC to be called away from the village at the end of his patrol there in order to provide a police presence in a nearby town centre when the pubs closed. In all, during the six-month trial period he visited the village 28 times and patrolled for four to five hours a week. He dealt with four incidents without Regular officers and assisted Regulars in two. He attended one Home Watch and five Parish Council meetings.

Scheme 2	% time
Solo foot patrol	31
Accompanied foot patrol	6
Mobile patrol	28
Visits to old people's homes	11
Schools	10
Parish Council meetings	3
Neighbourhood Watch	1
Other	10

Based on: 163 hours over 16 weeks
(= 10.2 hours per week on average)

Scheme 3	% time
Foot patrol	26
Mobile patrol	14
Paperwork	6
Dealing with detainees	6
Observations	5
Crime prevention	5
Community involvement	9
Parish Council	1
Special operations/ events	12
Training	3
Briefings/ meetings	3
Other	11

Based on: 70 hours over 17 weeks
(= 4.1 hours per week on average)

These figures suggest that something between one-quarter and one-third of the time spent on duty by these particular PSCs was taken up in foot patrol. Perhaps a little unexpected is the considerable amount of time which also appeared to have been spent on mobile patrol. The original intention of the PSC initiative was that very little time indeed should be spent in this way, and it is obviously important to guard against any tendency for PSCs to spend too much time out in cars. A problem here, as mentioned elsewhere, is that the training of Specials involves their going on accompanied patrol with regulars, and that such patrols often tend to be done in a vehicle.

To emphasise the importance of a clear strategy here it is worth noting a finding from the research which Warwickshire conducted into aspects of its policing service, including the work of Special Constables. In a survey of 111 of its Specials, prior to the setting up of the PSC scheme, it asked serving Specials what duties they would *most* like to do, and which they would *least* like to do. The most popular activity was found to be working *with a Regular shift*, followed by *mobile patrol in cars*. (This preference is also reflected in RPU's own earlier study of Special Constables.) By far the least popular activity was *involvement with Parish Councils*.

Such findings emphasize the need for great care to be taken to recruit into PSC work only those people with a disposition for the style and type of police work involved, rather than for more 'mainstream' uniformed patrol duties. They also emphasise again one of the basic dilemmas about PSC schemes: are PSCs to be trained and conditioned to take on the work - and, by extension, the values - of Regular policing; or are they, somehow, to be kept apart, so that they develop a different set of occupational styles and priorities? The latter approach may well have some advantages but, the more they follow it, the more difficult it may become to integrate them into the police organisation as a whole. But if they are not integrated, then their self-esteem and public credibility may both be at risk.

Apart from recruiting as PSCs people with a penchant for foot patrol work, managers and supervisors of PSC schemes should clearly make it a priority to minimise the amount of time the PSCs then spend in vehicles, and maximise their time on patrol work or in direct involvement with the community.

The views of local residents

Some people seemed confused about whether the job of the PSC was to provide a full range of police services within the village, or whether it was simply to provide a coordinating role - a link between the Regular police and the community.

Most people spoken to were despondent about the lack of a resident Regular police officer in their village and, on the whole, welcomed the idea of having a PSC as the 'next best thing' to this Regular police presence. But it was clear from the discussion groups that residents had serious doubts whether a PSC could provide them with an adequate substitute for a Regular resident officer, particularly where he did not live in the village itself. Unless he was a local some people felt that a PSC would not develop an adequate feeling for local needs.

There were two main concerns. First, it was recognised that, as a volunteer, a PSC could give only a small amount of time to policing the village: he was not 'on call 24 hours a day' as the old-style village bobby was felt to have been. Second, many people believed that Special Constables lacked the powers of 'real' police officers, particularly the power of arrest. Many were not aware that their PSC actually had these full police powers of arrest, rather than simply citizen's arrest powers. There was clearly a widespread misunderstanding as to their status and, thus, of their powers to deal with crime and disorder problems. This ignorance was directly related to the low expectations which many people expressed about their PSC scheme.

Strong feelings of discontent came from the residents of one of the schemes. Here, the provision of PSCs was seen by residents as not simply a 'second best' solution, but as a totally inadequate response to their problems. Those in the discussion groups held there in early June saw the PSC scheme as having failed so far to make any impact on the local community or its problems. Respondents with young families had not seen any evidence of the PSC's presence, and were cynical and angry about the scheme, viewing it as cosmetic and unlikely to produce anything worthwhile. Having seen the publicity at the start of the scheme they had believed, naively now they felt, that some help would be available to assist with the village's problems. One said:

> 'This is rubbish, we've got major problems here and they send us a part-time policeman. What a joke...'

Older respondents described their limited contact with the PSCs, although it became clear that some had met them and believed them to be Regular officers. This confusion may, possibly, have reduced the perceived impact of the scheme. Older residents certainly did not feel more effectively policed with the advent of the scheme, believing that the PSCs would not be available at night, when they would be most required, and so would make little impact on crime.

The teenage discussion group members appeared to be those most aware of the scheme's existence and most likely to have had some contact with the PSCs. They seemed, also, to be the most positive, feeling that PSCs might not display the prejudices and attitudes held by Regular police officers, and be able to interact with the young people of the village without alienating them in the way Regular officers were felt to.

Overall, the scheme was subjected to heavy criticism, with residents upset at what they saw as the ineffectual nature of what could have been a useful development. All were keen that PSCs should be resident in the village and could not imagine the job being undertaken by an outsider. The idea of a full-time, resident police officer was continually returned to, as were the problems and special needs of the village.

Many of those involved in interviews and group discussions referred simply to the 'Special Constable(s)' in their village, and did not use the 'Parish' prefix. This seemed to confuse some as to who was employing the PSCs and what their role was. Some also found it a little antiquated. There were suggestions that the title had associations with the church, or with Victorian times. Special Constables have been on the scene for many years; people are generally quite familiar with the title and seem happy to continue using it. Alternative titles suggested by group discussion members were: "Community Police Officer", "Rural Policeman", "Village Special Constable", or "Village Constable".

In the longer term, any confusions about terminology may be overcome by the recent introduction of the broader concept of the 'Neighbourhood' Constable though, for the moment, the 'Parish' prefix is being retained for many rural schemes. It would be helpful to establish just what these terms convey to the public in different parts of the country.

The different status of the volunteer PSC and the Regular 'village bobby' are reflected in the difficulties which people had experienced in communicating with PSCs. Police officers and public alike recognised that, because PSCs were not full-time paid employees, there was a limit to the amount of time and general availability that could be expected of them. Thus, there was caution from every scheme manager about letting the public know the telephone number of their PSC. If people required police services they were to ring 999 in emergency, or their local police station for less urgent matters. In many cases, however, there was confusion as to where the 'local' police station actually was; in some places there were as many as three possibilities.

Some contradiction may be found in promoting the idea of the PSC as, on the one hand, someone involved with the local community and, on the other, as a person who must not be approached except when walking the streets in a uniform. Where the PSC lives in the village and is well-known there it is inevitable that his address will be known. People could actually start calling at his door with their problems.

One obvious compromise between the need for access and the problem of personal privacy is to use an answering machine or message system which the public can call. This idea received only lukewarm support from the discussion groups but has, in fact, been used in some places. In one scheme this facility was made available to the public, but had resulted in only three messages per month so far. In another, a compromise arrangement had been made whereby the Regular police, the Parish Clerk and the Home Watch coordinators were given the number of the PSC's mobile phone, which had a message facility. The equipment and its use had cost over £300 over the six-month pilot period, but had carried a total of only six messages, five of them from police officers. The PSC had spent £60 simply calling to see whether there were any messages for him. There was some scepticism from the Regular police about this low usage of the scheme by Home Watch coordinators.

Low public usage of such message systems may simply reflect a lack of public awareness of them or of the PSC scheme in general. Usage might increase over time, though some people suggested that elderly people, in particular, could be reluctant to use such a device. Alternatively, there might have been no real demand or need for it.

Schools liaison

This was a function originally proposed for PSCs, but there has been only limited development so far. Schools Liaison is, of course, a well established specialist function within police forces, and most schools receive periodic visits from the Divisional/Area School Liaison Officer (SLO) who gives talks about road safety, going with strangers, crime prevention and so on.

So far, it seems that PSCs have been too busy developing basic patrol work and developing other contacts to get very involved with schools. There was no opposition to the idea of closer involvement with local schools and, in some forces, initial contacts had been made. There was some hesitation, though, about taking on too much of this before patrol work had become properly established.

Close contact with local primary schools does seem to be a fairly fundamental part of building a relationship with a community. Clearly, there is scope for PSCs to work more closely with local schools, if time can be found and their visits can be integrated with those of SLOs. A limitation here, though, is that many PSCs are working at their regular paid jobs during school hours.

The general issue of the behaviour of young people was clearly high on the agenda in most villages. In one area the village school was itself having problems with out-of-hours vandalism from older children (not its own pupils). But it was turning for help neither to the PSCs nor to the Regular police; both were seen as ineffective in the face of the problem, and a private security company was being called in instead.

Other proactive work

Three further areas of work with the public originally envisaged for PSCs were: *victim support; giving crime prevention advice; and advising neighbourhood and other watch schemes.* So far, there has been limited activity on these fronts. One PSC had held a Crime Prevention evening for residents and Neighbourhood Watch coordinators, and had done some follow-up work with victims. Other forces were thinking about pointing their PSCs in those directions, but it seemed to be agreed that the first priority was simply to establish visible patrol activity. If this can first be done then it will be time enough to move on to activities such as these, involving more proactive work.

One PSC had been in contact with his village's Home Watch head coordinator. But he had not been allowed to take over the police role in this scheme since the Section Commander felt the RBO had developed a good relationship with the coordinators which might be jeopardised by the PSC's involvement. Nor was the PSC able to give residents any crime prevention advice, as he was not trained to do so; only a number of Regular officers were qualified to give this advice. Fears were expressed that even advice given by a qualified officer could lead to legal action if the resident was then burgled. Requests to the Regular police for crime prevention advice were commonly met by posting a list of details on recommended security firms which would survey homes and fit locks.

3 Other responses to law and order problems

Parish Wardens

In addition to Parish Special Constable schemes, a number of Parish Warden schemes have been created around the country. One of these - based in the small Dorset town of Stalbridge - was examined in the RPU study.

This scheme, along with another at Broadwindsor, was run for six months by Dorset County Council, and was based broadly upon the original Home Office formulation mentioned at the beginning of this report. The Stalbridge scheme set out to emphasise: communication between the various parties involved in community safety; the promotion of security marking; and the support of Home Watch. These were all activities which it was felt needed greater support than they had been getting. It was not expected that the Warden would do patrol work, the emphasis being upon a coordination and communication role.

Unfortunately, although it looked feasible at the outset on paper, the experience of the Stalbridge scheme was not encouraging. But there were various reasons why this can be seen to have been the case. In this instance the person chosen as a Warden was already a Neighbourhood Watch Coordinator, and neither he nor others could actually see how his new role as a Warden could be much different from what he was already doing. Both the Parish Council and the local police seemed unclear as to what he was supposed to do in his new role. The Warden himself felt there were no new initiatives to develop in that role, and it was difficult for either him or others to say when he was acting as a NW coordinator and when as a Parish Warden.

Because the Warden's job involved no patrolling and because he did not seek publicity in any case, he seemed to have a very low profile within the local community. Thus, at the time of the RPU discussion groups halfway through the life of the scheme, nobody actually seemed aware of the existence of a Parish Warden. Public demands on his services as a Parish Warden were minimal.

The other Dorset Parish Warden scheme at Broadwindsor was different in that it achieved rather more local publicity, and it also involved a Warden who was not already involved in Home Watch. But, even so, local residents again seemed to have no more demand for the services of a Warden than did those in Stalbridge.

The Dorset experience highlights the need for a clearly defined role for a Warden that is agreed and understood by all those involved. Firm commitment is also required. It may be that Warden schemes elsewhere which include other features, such as an element of patrol work or closer involvement with the police, might fare somewhat better. Very thorough advance consultation and planning are certainly essential in setting up a Warden Scheme.

Community Force

In Sedgefield, Co Durham a different approach has been taken to the provision of a uniformed patrol presence. Here, in late 1993, the District Council set up its own uniformed 'Community Force' to patrol the streets on a 24-hour basis. The initial cost was some £180,000. Although similar in some ways to a commercial security patrol, the force is a department of the council, not a commercial company. It has its own control room and ten patrol officers, using mobile telephones, two-way radios and marked patrol cars. It came into full operation in February 1994.

The main objectives of the Community Force are described as being:

(i) To provide a community patrol which will increase public safety and reassure the public. (ii) To consult with local residents regarding anti-social problems in their area. (iii) To consult with local police regarding crime trends and problems, and how the Force can assist in combatting them. (iv) To provide advice and information to local residents on crime prevention. (v) To adopt a non-confrontational policy of observe and report.

Thus, the force exists to simply observe and report to the police anything suspicious, rather than to take any action themselves. Officers have no police powers of arrest. The Durham Constabulary is cautious in its attitude to the Community Force, but it has, nevertheless, helped in the training of the Force in relation to evidence gathering, scene of crime protection and bomb threat procedure.

During its first year of operation the force received several thousand calls from the public, and significant reductions in crime were recorded in the area. However, there is no evidence as to whether this can be attributed to the Community Force, or to the increased levels of patrol said to have been mounted at the same time by the Durham Constabulary - or to other factors entirely.

A report on the scheme and public reaction to it has been prepared at Sheffield University, based upon telephone interviews with a randomly selected sample of 360 local electors. High levels of awareness and visibility appear to have been achieved by the Force: seven out of ten of those interviewed said they had seen their vehicles. People said that they were generally happy to have the Sedgefield patrols in their streets, though they favoured patrols by Specials or other police officers even more. They were less happy, though, with the idea of patrols provided by private security companies.

Private security firms

In one of the scheme areas the Parish Council have, so far, found the PSC system to be an inadequate substitute for regular police patrol: as volunteers, the PSCs are simply not able to be available for long enough and at the times when there is most likely to be disorder taking place. The answer to this has been the employment of a private security firm which now provides a patrol on Friday and Saturday evenings in the playing fields and recreation ground. It has just been decided to extend this to some hours during the week as well. The PSCs are aware of the Council's actions and are somewhat disappointed that they are unable to satisfy the perceived needs of the village.

In another area the Parish Council had been approached by a private security firm seeking to establish itself in the area. It was already providing surveillance for some local residents, but the Council decided not to employ the firm on behalf of the community as a whole.

Observers

Since February 1994 Glenfield Parish in Leicestershire has had its own team of 60 'observers', coordinated by a Special Constable and supported by the Leicestershire Constabulary. They have no equipment other than an official identity badge, a notebook and a torch. Their role is simply to observe, often during the course of their daily passage around the village, walking their dog or going to the shops. They report to their coordinator or, as appropriate, directly to the police. They are not encouraged to become directly involved in anything, simply to provide additional information to the police, who will then take any immediate or longer term action judged to be necessary.

The Observers receive training from the Police Community Unit in the purpose of the scheme and the functions it involves, e.g. correct use of the telephone, location of telephone kiosks and other contact points, how to submit reports, how to go about their patrol and personal safety.

The role of the Special Constable coordinating the scheme is to:

- Receive log books each month and complete a summary of patrols undertaken.

- Forward this summary to the Parish Council and to the Police Community Unit Liaison Officer.

- Pass any information received to the Liaison Officer, and summarise this information to the Parish Council each month.

- Provide identification for patrolling observers.

- Maintain a list of observers and copy this to the police.

- Maintain a log of areas receiving regular patrols.

- Ensure that adequate points are available on each area of patrol.

- Liaise with regular beat officers regarding street patrols.

- Liaise with Neighbourhood Watch coordinators.

The Observers scheme operates in parallel, to some extent, with the local Neighbourhood Watch scheme, though there are links between the two at coordinator level. In their first seven months the Observers completed, between them, an average of 115 hours of patrol per month. During this time, three incidents had been reported directly to the police, but there is little further information available to date about the operation and success of the scheme. A favourable response from the community has been reported by the Observers.

4 Conclusions

This report has reviewed the setting up and first months of operation of Parish Special Constable (PSC) schemes. A number of schemes across the country were monitored, with particular attention paid to those within four force areas. In addition, one Parish Warden scheme was examined, and the report also refers to other schemes for providing patrols in local communities.

Progress

Although nominally starting at the beginning of 1994, many PSC schemes only really became established later in the year; and some had not achieved full implementation by the end of 1994. As a result, at the time of writing, information about many schemes was not yet available. Even for schemes which were in place at an early stage it is important not to make premature judgements about their success or failure: such initiatives take time to become established and bear fruit. This view was endorsed by all those involved in the running of schemes.

Of the four PSC schemes examined in detail during 1994, one has now closed down and three continue. The *Yetminster* scheme was closed down after its nominal six months pilot period. The Regular police seemed to be doing an adequate job in the village, and had remained fairly active there even after PSCs were appointed. One of the two PSC appointed left half-way through the six months, and the other at the end. He had often been used for policing duties elsewhere, and found limited interest in the PSC scheme.

The local police view was that the scheme did have some good effects: local residents were said to have appreciated seeing an officer patrolling the village and would have liked him to continue doing so. At the same time there were concerns about the staffing implications of expanding the scheme or setting up further schemes in the area.

Ironville had some of the worst law and order problems of the four villages, and many residents felt that the PSC scheme was quite inadequate in the face of them. Some young people did, however, think that PSCs might be more sympathetic to them than Regular officers. In some regards the scheme was well organised and supported by police management, but it seems to have been kept at some distance from the Regulars, and this did not help build up effective links. The local Council was generally supportive, although one PSC felt that some councillors were expecting too much of him. The main problem was turnover in personnel: two Specials started; then one dropped out and was replaced; then the other original officer left. The scheme continues, but needs some consolidation in this regard.

Pembury is a large village and six PSCs were originally allocated to it. One of these left to join the Regulars; two of those remaining currently carry much of the load. This group have good backing from police management. The Parish Council are supportive up to a point, but have turned to a private security company to address the particular problems they have with vandalism to council property. Once the PSCs have gained more experience they may develop into a useful team.

Of the four schemes, the one which most closely approximates the 'ideal' model of PSC policing originally envisaged is Sleights. This has had the benefit of a mature and experienced Special Constable, already living in the village and ready to take on the PSC role. Both police managers and local residents felt that his living in the village was important, though some residents suggested that his PSC role might impinge too much upon his private life because of this.

The *Sleights* PSC has good support, both from the police and the community. The Parish Council back him, but take a low-key approach to influencing his priorities and activities. He has been, and remains, active and, although working single-handed, seems determined to continue delivering a service to his community. If the Sleights scheme continues to be successful, the police hope to recruit further PSCs to cover other villages in the division.

The Parish Warden scheme in *Stalbridge* made very little progress and is now defunct, along with the other two similar schemes started in Dorset at the same time. Its main problem seemed to be a lack of a distinct identity and purpose: there was little it seemed able to do which Neighbourhood Watch could not accomplish.

Personalities

As with most organisational innovations, the key factors in getting a scheme into operation and keeping it running are the personality and commitment of both the scheme organiser and the person(s) doing the job in the front line. At the same time, it must be recognised that even the most suitable people can only make things work within an environment which is sufficiently supportive, from a social, organisational and resource point of view.

It has been widely recognised that not all those currently joining the Special Constabulary are suitable for PSC roles. What most forces have sought has been people of fairly mature demeanour and approach, resident locally, with interests in community policing, and without ambitions to get involved in the more 'exciting' aspects of policing or to join the regular force. Such a person, it was felt, would fit most easily into the slightly avuncular 'village bobby' role and become accepted into a rural community.

In practice, a variety of people, men and women, had become involved in and seemed to have taken to PSC work. Some women, for example, who worked varied hours at their regular jobs, found it convenient to do daytime patrol or community contact work. For others, with daytime jobs or more fixed hours, this was difficult. The potential isolation of PSC work did, however, pose difficulties for most people; those working single-handed in a village were especially vulnerable here, and expressed their concerns.

The PSC role

PSCs are both members of their local communities and, while on duty, uniformed police officers. Sometimes, local people are not quite clear which they are meant to be. Some parish councils seemed reluctant to become very deeply involved in PSC schemes, and left the police force to take most of the initiative. This creates a danger that the police side of the balance will tend to be emphasised and the element of partnership given less attention. Unless every opportunity is taken from both sides to strengthen this element, it will be difficult for PSCs to work as a genuine link between police forces and communities. Time and experience will determine how the PSC role develops in individual cases. Ultimately, it will be determined by the balance of inputs from police forces, local councils, local residents and PSCs themselves.

In establishing this role, PSCs have to work with communities which are changing in their nature; some of the assumptions about how they might capitalise upon local social networks, hierarchies and patterns of influence need to be questioned. Rather than being rural, many villages now have much more of an urban or suburban character. The vicar, the doctor, the schoolmaster and the village policeman are no longer looked up to as the key figures and leaders in a village. PSCs have a difficult task in trying to identify who, if anyone, does now speak for the community, and what form that community actually takes.

Public reactions

One measure of the success of PSC schemes will be simply how long it takes for local residents to become aware of the schemes and the presence of PSCs. Their work needs to become as well-known locally as that of the Regular police is now. In this regard different schemes seemed to be at different stages.

Many local people saw PSCs as a second best option for their village, and as 'policing on the cheap'. In every village people said they would much prefer a 'real' police officer living in a police house in the village. They did not feel that an adequate police service could be provided by part-timers working for nothing.

People clearly often underestimated the powers of Special Constables. This may have resulted partly from a lack of the right sort of publicity, and partly from Specials' own lack of opportunity to use those powers. Until people come to realize that Specials do have full police powers of arrest, they are unlikely to take the idea of the PSC very seriously.

Members of the public did not seem to relate well to the title "*Parish* Special Constable", and felt more at home with the longer established term "Special Constable". The adoption of the more generic term "Neighbourhood Constable" by the Home Office may help here, though some forces seem keen to keep the originally agreed "Parish" prefix for rural schemes.

The 'image' of local policing

In some areas redundant local police offices are available for the use of PSCs and provide a useful base of operations. But the rather down-at-heel appearance of some of them fails to present policing in its best light in local eyes, and gives the impression that it is being neglected. If the exteriors (and interiors) of these buildings could be refurbished and more clearly identified as a place of contact with the police, then this could help to increase both the visibility and the status of the PSC in local eyes.

Integration with Regular policing

While some Regular police officers have been positive and appreciative of the work of PSCs, others are sceptical or even hostile. This kind of suspicion is best avoided by consulting and involving Regular officers as closely as possible in the planning and operation of the schemes. The aim must be to establish close working relationships and maximise the integration of

Specials and Regulars on a day-to-day basis. Unless this can be achieved, the danger is that PSCs will be isolated, both from other Specials and from Regulars.

Other forms of community patrol

The PSC system is only one of various approaches to the provision of local patrols. A Sheffield University study of public reactions to the Sedgefield Community Force suggests, though, that PSCs - or, at least, some other publicly run scheme - may be the solution most commonly preferred. Commercial security patrols were the least favoured option. In one of the areas studied for this report a commercial security firm was, however, being brought in to trouble spots on council land despite the presence of a developing PSC scheme.

Other approaches to the use of volunteers to supplement Regular policing include the use of non-uniformed civilians as 'Wardens', 'Observers' or police station staff. This report has looked briefly at these. The one Warden scheme studied was a failure largely, it seems, because of its almost total lack of public visibility. The Observer scheme is still at too early a stage to judge its viability. In both cases the practical issues are somewhat different from those involved in PSC schemes and have not been considered at any length.

Judging effectiveness

There are two issues involved in any evaluation. First, how well is a programme implemented? Second, what effects does it actually produce? This report has looked at aspects of the first. The latter can only be addressed after some time and, even then, it will be difficult to find clear answers, because the activities of PSCs are but one of many things happening in any village which are likely to influence crime and disorder. Thus, for example, the Regular police may increase their presence in some places at the same time as PSCs appear on the scene. Or, particular offenders may move away from the village or be arrested for reasons unconnected with the level of visible police presence there. Apart from such factors, the numbers of crimes and incidents occurring in a village may be very small statistically, so that even if there is some change it is impossible to say whether this represents a significant change, let alone an effect of the PSC scheme.

The most thorough measures of public response to PSC schemes would be provided by systematic surveys of local residents, conducted before and some time after the start of a scheme. These could assess awareness and understanding of the scheme, and concerns about and experiences with crime and disorder. The RPU did not have sufficient resources to conduct full sample surveys, though some forces managed to run such surveys themselves.

5 Recommendations

- In setting up future schemes local people should be consulted as widely and as early as possible. If Parish Councils are to be involved in doing this, then they must be given adequate time. Too much haste to get things moving was blamed for teething problems and misunderstandings in some schemes.

- Local media should be carefully briefed, to avoid misunderstandings about the role of PSCs being passed on to the public. Realistic expectations must be established about how much time they will be able to provide and what they may or may not be able to achieve.

- Suggestions were found of a considerable public ignorance about the legal powers of Special Constables. A better understanding about the powers of PSCs must be created if their credibility is to be established and maintained.

- Great care must be taken to get the right sort of people for the job. Both its rewards and difficulties must be made clear to potential applicants. At least one scheme has already closed partly because of a lack of enthusiasm on the part of the PSC.

- PSCs cannot be recruited directly from the community and put on duty without adequate training and preparation. This means either that a new scheme must wait until this has been done before it can become active, or that trained and experienced personnel must be found to staff it from within the existing body of the Special Constabulary.

- Where existing Specials are recruited into PSC work, care must be taken to select those who are interested in working in a community policing mode rather than in incident-response mode.

- The training of Specials for the PSC role needs careful thought. At the moment this training sometimes involves taking new recruits away from the village situation, to work either in towns or on vehicle patrol. It would be better if ways could be found for more training to be done in the village: experienced officers might be 'brought to' the PSCs, rather than the reverse.

- Supervisors must take all steps possible to minimise the time PSCs spend on mobile patrol and maximise the time they spend either on foot patrol or in direct contact with their community.

- The precise job title to be used by Specials working in villages or other neighbourhoods should be carefully considered. The 'Parish' prefix was not well accepted by the public. People may prefer the more generic 'Neighbourhood' designation now proposed by the Home Office, and this should be tested.

- More PSC patrols in daylight hours would increase their visibility and help provide public reassurance. This consideration, plus the need for school visits to be made during the day, suggests that forces should recruit some PSCs who can be available during the day for at least part of their duty time.

- It should be acknowledged that working alone in a village may be bad for a PSC's morale and effectiveness. Such individuals need particularly strong support and encouragement, from both the police force and the local community, if they are to maintain their momentum and not become isolated.

- Closer integration is needed between PSCs and the Regular force, particularly local beat officers, so that PSCs feel part of the police organisation. Efforts need to be coordinated and planned. There needs to be more regular contact and exchange of information and advice in both directions.

- PSCs could benefit from closer contact with other Specials. It is important here to build upon existing Special Constabulary supervision and management structures, strengthening and developing these as necessary.

- In the longer term, the way to improve PSC patrol coverage and continuity of staffing, while reducing the demands on individual volunteers, could be to set up a small team of PSCs in a village. Team spirit can benefit morale, and it might also be possible to avoid boredom by rotating individual Specials between PSC and traditional section work. This could strengthen links with the rest of the Regular force and the Special Constabulary.

- Before getting involved in crime prevention advice, Neighbourhood Watch or other proactive tasks, PSCs must be established in their patrol work and have received adequate training. This will take time.

- The School Liaison role of PSCs needs to be clarified and, possibly, more formally stated, showing how it fits in with that of existing School Liaison Officers. Extra training may also be needed before PSCs can make a good contribution.

- Radio communication problems need to be resolved as far as is technically possible, so that PSCs have adequate means of communication with the local control room.

- The provision of a base from which PSCs can operate has distinct advantages, especially where several work in one village. The premises should be well maintained and clearly identified as a police office, so as to present a favourable public image.

- The means by which the public can contact PSCs must be decided and then publicised. More guidance could be provided as to how information is to be relayed to the police via the PSC. Refurbished police offices could have letter boxes and notices giving information and telephone numbers.

- The longer term impact of PSC schemes upon crime, disorder and public perceptions of policing needs to be monitored.

References

Home Office (1992). *Police Activity Sampling: Manual of guidance.* London: Home Office.

Home Office (1993). *Notifiable Offences: England and Wales, 1992.* Home Office Statistical Bulletin 9/93. London: Home Office.

Mirrlees-Black, C. and Byron, C. (1994). *Special Considerations: issues for the management and organisation of the volunteer police.* Research and Planning Unit Paper No 88. London: Home Office.

Reiner, R. (1992). *The Politics of the Police (2nd ed).* London: Wheatsheaf-Harvester.

Publications

List of Research and Planning Unit Publications

The Research and Planning Unit (previously the Research Unit) has been publishing its work since 1955, and a list of reports for the last three years is provided below. A **full** list of publications is available on request from the Research and Planning Unit.

Home Office Research Studies (HORS)

125.   **Magistrates' court or Crown Court? Mode of trial decisions and sentencing.** Carol Hedderman and David Moxon. 1992. vii + 53pp. (0 11 341036 0).

126.   **Developments in the use of compensation orders in magistrates' courts since October 1988.** David Moxon, John Martin Corkery and Carol Hedderman. 1992. x + 48pp. (0 11 341042 5).

127.   **A comparative study of firefighting arrangements in Britain, Denmark, the Netherlands and Sweden.** John Graham, Simon Field, Roger Tarling and Heather Wilkinson. 1992. x + 57pp. (0 11 341043 3).

128.   **The National Prison Survey 1991: main findings.** Roy Walmsley, Liz Howard and Sheila White. 1992. xiv + 82pp. (0 11 341051 4).

129.   **Changing the Code: police detention under the revised PACE Codes of Practice.** David Brown, Tom Ellis and Karen Larcombe. 1992. viii + 122pp. (0 11 341052 2).

130.   **Car theft: the offender's perspective.** Roy Light, Claire Nee and Helen Ingham. 1993. x + 89pp. (0 11 341069 7).

131.   **Housing, Community and Crime: The Impact of the Priority Estates Project.** Janet Foster and Timothy Hope with assistance from Lizanne Dowds and Mike Sutton. 1993. xi + 118pp. (0 11 341078 6).

132. **The 1992 British Crime Survey.** Pat Mayhew, Natalie Aye Maung and Catriona Mirrlees-Black. 1993. xiii + 206pp. (0 11 341094 8).

133. **Intensive Probation in England and Wales: an evaluation.** George Mair, Charles Lloyd, Claire Nee and Rae Sibbett. 1994. xiv + 143pp. (0 11 341114 6).

134. **Contacts between Police and Public: findings from the 1992 British Crime Survey.** Wesley G Skogan. 1995. ix + 93pp. (0 11 341115 4).

135. **Policing low-level disorder : Police use of Section 5 of the Public Order Act 1986.** David Brown and Tom Ellis. 1994. ix + 69pp. (0 11 341116 2).

136. **Explaining reconviction rates: A critical analysis.** Charles Lloyd, George Mair and Mike Hough. 1995. xiv + 103pp. (0 11 341117 0).

137. **Case Screening by the Crown Prosecution Service: How and why cases are terminated.** Debbie Crisp and David Moxon. 1995. viii + 66pp. (0 11 341137 5).

138. **Public Interest Case Assessment Schemes.** Debbie Crisp, Claire Whittaker and Jessica Harris. 1995. x + 58pp. (0 11 341139 1).

139. **Policing domestic violence in the 1990s.** Sharon Grace. 1995. x + 74pp. (0 11 341140 5).

140. **Young people, victimisation and the police: British Crime Survey findings on experiences and attitudes of 12 to 15 year olds.** Natalie Aye Maung. xii + 140pp. (Not yet published)

141. **The Settlement of refugees in Britain.** Jenny Carey-Wood, Karen Duke, Valerie Karn and Tony Marshall. 1995. xii + 133pp. (0 11 341145 6).

142. **Vietnamese Refugees since 1982.** Karen Duke and Tony Marshall. 1995. x + 62pp. (0 11 341147 2).

Research and Planning Unit Papers (RPUP)

65. **Offending while on bail: a survey of recent studies.** Patricia M. Morgan. 1992.

66. **Juveniles sentenced for serious offences: a comparison of regimes in Young Offender Institutions and Local Authority Community Homes.** John Ditchfield and Liza Catan. 1992.

67. **The management and deployment of police armed response vehicles.** Peter Southgate. 1992.

68. **Using psychometric personality tests in the selection of firearms officers.** Catriona Mirrlees-Black. 1992.

69. **Bail information schemes: practice and effect.** Charles Lloyd. 1992.

70. **Crack and cocaine in England and Wales.** Joy Mott (editor). 1992.

71. **Rape: from recording to conviction.** Sharon Grace, Charles Lloyd and Lorna J. F. Smith. 1992.

72. **The National Probation Survey 1990.** Chris May. 1993.

73. **Public satisfaction with police services.** Peter Southgate and Debbie Crisp. 1993.

74. **Disqualification from driving: an effective penalty?** Catriona Mirrlees-Black. 1993.

75. **Detention under the Prevention of Terrorism (Temporary Provisions) Act 1989: Access to legal advice and outside contact.** David Brown. 1993.

76. **Panel assessment schemes for mentally disordered offenders.** Carol Hedderman. 1993.

77. **Cash-limiting the probation service: a case study in resource allocation.** Simon Field and Mike Hough. 1993.

78. **The probation response to drug misuse.** Claire Nee and Rae Sibbitt. 1993.

79 **Approval of rifle and target shooting clubs: the effects of the new and revised criteria.** John Martin Corkery. 1993.

80. **The long-term needs of victims: A review of the literature.** Tim Newburn. 1993.

81. **The welfare needs of unconvicted prisoners.** Diane Caddle and Sheila White. 1994.

82. **Racially motivated crime: a British Crime Survey analysis.** Natalie Aye Maung and Catriona Mirrlees-Black. 1994.

83. **Mathematical models for forecasting Passport demand.** Andy Jones and John MacLeod. 1994.

84. **The theft of firearms.** John Corkery. 1994.

85. **Equal opportunities and the Fire Service.** Tom Bucke. 1994.

86. **Drug Education Amongst Teenagers: a 1992 British Crime Survey Analysis.** Lizanne Dowds and Judith Redfern. 1995.

87. **Group 4 Prisoner Escort Service: a survey of customer satisfaction.** Claire Nee. 1994.

88. **Special Considerations: Issues for the Management and Organisation of the Volunteer Police.** Catriona Mirrlees-Black and Carole Byron. 1995.

89. **Self-reported drug misuse in England and Wales: findings from the 1992 British Crime Survey.** Joy Mott and Catriona Mirrlees-Black. 1995.

90. **Improving bail decisions: the bail process project, phase 1.** John Burrows, Paul Henderson and Patricia Morgan. 1995.

91. **Practitioners' views of the Criminal Justice Act: a survey of criminal justice agencies.** George Mair and Chris May. 1995

92. **Obscene, threatening and other troublesome telephone calls to women in England and Wales: 1982-1992.** Wendy Buck, Michael Chatterton and Ken Pease. 1995.

Research Findings

1. **Magistrates' court or Crown Court? Mode of trial decisions and their impact on sentencing.** Carol Hedderman and David Moxon. 1992.

2. **Surveying crime: findings from the 1992 British Crime Survey.** Pat Mayhew and Natalie Aye Maung. 1992.

3.   **Car Theft: the offenders' perspective.** Claire Nee. 1993.

4.   **The National Prison survey 1991: main findings.** Roy Walmsley, Liz Howard and Sheila White. 1993.

5.   **Changing the Code: Police detention under the revised PACE codes of practice.** David Brown, Tom Ellis and Karen Larcombe. 1993.

6.   **Rifle and pistol target shooting clubs: The effects of new approval criteria.** John M. Corkery. 1993.

7.   **Self-reported drug misuse in England and Wales. Main findings from the 1992 British Crime Survey.** Joy Mott and Catriona Mirrlees-Black. 1993.

8.   **Findings from the International Crime Survey.** Pat Mayhew. 1994.

9   **Fear of Crime: Findings from the 1992 British Crime Survey.** Catriona Mirrlees-Black and Natalie Aye Maung. 1994.

10. **Does the Criminal Justice system treat men and women differently?** Carol Hedderman and Mike Hough. 1994.

11. **Participation in Neighbourhood Watch: Findings from the 1992 British Crime Survey.** Lizanne Dowds and Pat Mayhew. 1994.

12. **Explaining Reconviction Rates: A Critical Analysis.** Charles Lloyd, George Mair and Mike Hough. 1995.

13. **Equal opportunities and the Fire Service.** Tom Bucke. 1994.

14. **Trends in Crime: Findings from the 1994 British Crime Survey.** Pat Mayhew, Catriona Mirrlees-Black and Natalie Aye Maung. 1994.

15. **Intensive Probation in England and Wales: an evaluation.** George Mair, Charles Lloyd, Claire Nee and Rae Sibbett. 1995.

16. **The settlement of refugees in Britain.** Jenny Carey-Wood, Karen Duke, Valerie Karn and Tony Marshall. 1995.

17. **Young people, victimisation and the police: British Crime Survey findings on experiences and attitudes of 12 to 15 year olds.** Natalie Aye Maung. (Not yet published)

18. **Vietnamese Refugees since 1982.** Karen Duke and Tony Marshall. 1995.

19. **Supervision of Restricted Patients in the Community.** Dell and Grounds. (Not yet published)

20. **Videotaping children's evidence: an evaluation.** Graham Davies, Clare Wilson, Rebecca Mitchell and John Milsom. 1995.

Research Bulletin

The Research Bulletin is published twice each year and contains short articles on recent research. Research Bulletin No. 37 was published recently.

Occasional Papers

Coping with a crisis: the introduction of three and two in a cell. T. G. Weiler. 1992.

Psychiatric Assessment at the Magistrates' Court. Philip Joseph. 1992.

Measurement of caseload weightings in magistrates' courts. Richard J. Gadsden and Graham J. Worsdale. 1992.

The CDE of scheduling in magistrates' courts. John W. Raine and Michael J. Willson. 1992.

Employment opportunities for offenders. David Downes. 1993.

Sex offenders: a framework for the evaluation of community-based treatment. Mary Barker and Rod Morgan. 1993.

Suicide attempts and self-injury in male prisons. Alison Liebling and Helen Krarup. 1993.

Measurement of caseload weightings associated with the Children Act. Richard J. Gadsden and Graham J. Worsdale. 1994. (Available from the RPU Information Section.)

Managing difficult prisoners: The Lincoln and Hull special units. Professor Keith Bottomley, Professor Norman Jepson, Mr Kenneth Elliott and Dr Jeremy Coid. 1994. (Available from RPU Information Section).

The Nacro diversion iniative for mentally disturbed offenders: an account and an evaluation. Home Office, NACRO and Mental Health Foundation. 1994. (Available from RPU Information Section).

Probation Motor Projects in England and Wales. J P Martin and Douglas Martin. 1994.

Community-based treatment of sex offenders: an evaluation of seven treatment programmes. R Beckett, A Beech, D Fisher and A S Fordham. 1994.

Videotaping children's evidence: an evaluation. Graham Davies, Clare Wilson, Rebecca Mitchell and John Milsom. 1995

Books

Analysing Offending. Data, Models and Interpretations. Roger Tarling. 1993. viii + 203pp. (0 11 341080 8).

Requests for Publications

Home Office Research Studies from 143 onwards, *Research and Planning Unit Papers, Research Findings, the Research and Planning Unit Programme and Research Bulletins* are available on request from the Information Section, Home Office Research and Planning Unit, Room 278, 50 Queen Anne's Gate, London SW1H 9AT. Telephone: 0171 273 2084 (answering machine).

Occasional Papers can be purchased from: Home Office, Publications Unit, 50 Queen Anne's Gate, London SW1 9AT. Telephone: 0171 273 2302

Home Office Research Studies prior to 143 can be purchased from:

HMSO Publications Centre
(Mail, fax and telephone orders only)
PO Box 276, London SW8 5DT
Telephone orders: 0171-873 9090
General enquiries: 0171-873 0011
(queuing system in operation for both numbers)
Fax orders: 0171-873 8200

And also from HMSO Bookshops